Handy New Jersey Genealogy Handbook

I0450654

By Gary L. Morris

©2015 Gary L. Morris

ISBN-13: 978-1507523926

ISBN-10: 1507523920

Table of Contents

Notes

Genealogical Research in New Jersey

There are many genealogical records and resources available for tracing your family history in New Jersey. Because there are so many records held at many different locations, tracking down the records for your ancestor can be an ominous task. Don't worry though, we know just where they are, and we'll show you which records you'll need, while helping you to understand:

1. What they are
2. Where to find them
3. How to use them

These records can be found both online and off, so we'll introduce you to online websites, indexes and databases, as well as brick-and-mortar repositories and other institutions that will help with your research in New Jersey. So that you will have a more comprehensive understanding of these records, we have provided a brief history of the "Garden State" to illustrate what type of records may have been generated during specific time periods. That information will assist you in pinpointing times and locations on which to focus the search for your New Jersey ancestors and their records.

A Brief History of New Jersey

Native Americans arrived in the area between the Hudson and Delaware rivers about 6,000 years ago. They were a peaceful, family oriented agricultural group who clung rigidly to a tradition that a pot of food must always be warm on the fire to welcome strangers. Giovanni da Verrazano was the first European explorer to reach New Jersey in 1524. In 1609 an English captain sailing under a Dutch flag, Henry Hudson, sailed along the New Jersey shore and into Sandy Hook Bay, establishing Dutch claims to the area. A trading post was established at Bergen, the site of present day Jersey City in 1618.

Despite a series of treaties deemed fair by the Swedish, Dutch, and English settlers, the Native Americans soon lost most of their land; traded for trinkets, guns, and alcohol. The guns and alcohol, combined with smallpox nearly wiped out the Native Americans, and when a treaty was signed establishing an Indian reservation in 1758, only a few hundred natives remained.

I March of 1664 the English seized control of the area when King Charles II granted his brother James, the Duke of York a tract of land from the Connecticut River to the Delaware River. James then deeded the area, which he named New Jersey, to his court friends John Berkeley, 1st Baron Berkeley of Stratton, and Sir George Carteret, who became proprietors of the land, owning it outright and having the right to govern its people.

New Jersey was subsequently divided into two regions, East Jersey and West Jersey, the east being settles by mostly Puritans, while Quakers were the majority to settle in the west. By the time of the American Revolution the colony was divided in both political and religious belief, though the dissent between Loyalists and Revolutionists was the most obvious.

Because of the influence of governor at the time William Franklin, the illegitimate son of Benjamin Franklin, the initial response from New Jersey to join the fight for independence was somewhat delayed. The state did however, in June of 1776, send five new delegates to the Continental Congress, all of whom voted for the Declaration of Independence.

The role of New Jersey in the Revolutionary War was a prominent and pivotal one, George Washington and his troops making their winter headquarters in the state three times during the first four years of the war, and major battles being fought in the region. During the war many of New Jersey's towns had been ravaged by armies from both sides, and the state languished upon its completion. New Jersey did however; support the cause for the federation of states with equal representation in a single legislative body which would eventually become the U.S. Senate.

By the 1830's canals and railways had invigorated the state, and a course of industrialization and urbanization began. The iron mines which sprung up around the canals found markets in major cities like Philadelphia and Boston, while weaving and dyeing mills prospered in Paterson, propelling Newark to become the first incorporated city in the state in 1836. Factories sprung up along the railways due to easy access to coal delivery, while the railways also helped to establish the states tourism industry by delivering passengers to the Jersey Shore.

The state was split bitterly by the Civil War, Democrats opposing the fight because of their lucrative ties to southern markets. The state fulfilled its obligations to the Union cause however, and sent its full quota of troops into battle. More important were the armaments and equipment supplied by the state's factories, though with the war's end, New Jersey stubbornly opposed the 13th, 14th, and 15th Amendments. Finally in 1870, blacks were given the right to vote.

Important Dates in New Jersey History

1618 – Dutch trading post established at Bergen

1640 – First Swedish settlements founded at Cape May and Raccoon Creek

1641 – First English settlement founded at Salem Creek

1664 – Established as a proprietary English colony

1666 – Newark founded by Puritans

1674 – Divided into East and West Jersey

1702 – East and West Jersey unite to form single province

1766 – Rutgers University founded

1776 – First State Constitution adopted

1787 – Third state to ratify U.S. Constitution

1790 – First state to sign Bill of Rights

1836 – Newark becomes first incorporated city

1870 – Black's given right to vote

Famous Battles Fought in New Jersey

Five major battles were fought in New Jersey during the revolutionary War, the most important being the **Battle of Trenton** on 26 December 1776 and the **Battle of Monmouth** on 28 June 1778.

Many other battles took place in New Jersey territory during the Revolutionary War due to its strategic significance, and for a comprehensive history you can visit the **Revolutionary War History in New Jersey** website.

These battle accounts that exist can be very effective in uncovering the military records of your ancestor. They can tell you what regiments fought in which battles, and often include the names and ranks of many officers and enlisted men.

Battle of Trenton: http://www.britishbattles.com/battle-trenton.htm

Battle of Monmouth:
http://www.wpi.edu/academics/military/monmouth.html

Revolutionary War History in New Jersey:
http://www.doublegv.com/ggv/

Common New Jersey Genealogical Issues and Resources to Overcome Them

Boundary Changes: Boundary changes are a common obstacle when researching New Jersey ancestors. You could be searching for an ancestor's record in one county when in fact it is stored in a different one due to historical county boundary changes.

The **Atlas of Historical County Boundaries** can help you to overcome that problem. It provides a chronological listing of every boundary change that has occurred in the history of New Jersey.

Atlas of Historical County Boundaries:
http://publications.newberry.org/ahcbp/documents/NJ_Consolidated _Chronology.htm#Consolidated_Chronology

Name Changes: Surname changes, variations, and misspellings can complicate genealogical research. It is important to check all spelling variations. Soundex, a program that indexes names by sound, is a useful first step, but you can't rely on it completely as some name variations result in different Soundex codes. The surnames could be different, but the first name may be different too. You can also find records filed under initials, middle names, and nicknames as well, so you will need to **get creative with surname variations** and spellings in order to cover all the possibilities. For help with surname variations read our instructional article on **How to Use Soundex**.

get creative with surname variations:
http://obituarieshelp.org/blog/?p=634

How to Use Soundex: http://obituarieshelp.org/blog/?p=505

New Jersey Genealogical Organizations and Archives

Genealogical resources include not only records, but the organizations that house them, or can direct you to them. These institutions include: *Archives, Libraries, Genealogical Societies, Family History Centers, Universities, Churches, and Museums.*

Following are links to their websites, their physical addresses, and a summary of the records you can find there.

Archives and Libraries

New Jersey Division of Archives and Records Management – vital records, census records, land and estate records, tax records, military records, court records, naturalization records, historical newspapers collection

225 West State Street
Trenton, New Jersey 08625-0307
Telephone: 609-292-6260

New Jersey Division of Archives and Records Management:
http://www.nj.gov/state/archives/index.html

National Archives - Northeast Region - Census Records, Naturalization Records, Passenger Arrival Lists, Canadian Border Entry Records, Customs Records, Draft, Military Service, and Pension and Bounty Land Application Files, Chinese Exclusion Act Case Files, Freedmen's Bureau and Records Pertaining to African American Families, Dawes Commission Final Cards of the Five Civilized Tribes, Vital Records

201 Varick Street
12th Floor
New York, New York 10014
Telephone: Toll-free 866-840-1752 or 212-401-1620
Fax: 212-401-1638

National Archives - Northeast Region:
http://www.archives.gov/nyc/public/genealogy.html

New Jersey State Library - genealogies, maps, church records, local histories, city directories, legislative reports, legal digests, periodicals, federal censuses of the eastern states, New Jersey state censuses, historical New Jersey newspapers

185 West State Street
(mailing address: P.O. Box 520)
Trenton, New Jersey 08625-0520
Telephone: 609-278-2640
Fax: 609-278-2647
E-Mail: refdesk@njstatelib.org

New Jersey State Library:
http://slic.njstatelib.org/library_collections/genealogy_and_local_his
tory

Rutgers University Library – records deposited by the Genealogical Society of New Jersey and the New Jersey State Society of the Daughters of the American Revolution, collection includes; cemetery inscriptions, family Bible records, county marriage records, and much more

Special Collections and University Archives
169 College Avenue
New Brunswick, NJ, 08901
Tel: 848-932-6000
Email: rbecker@rulmail.rutgers.edu

Rutgers University Library:
http://www.libraries.rutgers.edu/rul/libs/scua/genealogy/genealogy.s
html

New Jersey Genealogical and Historical Societies

Genealogical and historical societies have access to extensive catalogues of genealogical data. They are also able to offer expert guidance for genealogical researchers. Many members are professional genealogists who are most willing to share their expertise in finding ancestors.

New Jersey Historical Society Library - books, pamphlets, manuscripts, maps, census microfilms, indexed genealogy manuscript collections, and more

52 Park Place
Newark, New Jersey 07102
Telephone: 973-596-8500
Fax: 973-596-6957

New Jersey Historical Society Library:
http://www.jerseyhistory.org/librarymain.html

Gloucester County Historical Society Library - extensive collection of census records, vital records, maps, church records, local histories, city directories, genealogical charts, and more

17 Hunter Street
Woodbury, New Jersey 08096-4605
Telephone: 856-845-4771

Gloucester County Historical Society Library:
http://www.rootsweb.ancestry.com/~njgchs/Library.html

Genealogical Society of New Jersey – cemetery records, gravestone transcriptions, military records, Emigrant Register, family histories, military records

PO Box 1476
Trenton, NJ 08607-1476

Genealogical Society of New Jersey:
http://www.rootsweb.ancestry.com/~njgsnj/collectionguide.html

Additional Resources

New Jersey Mailing Lists

Mailing lists are internet based facilities that use email to distribute a single message to all who subscribe to it. When information on a particular surname, new records, or any other important genealogy information related to the mailing list topic becomes available, the subscribers are alerted to it. Joining a mailing list is an excellent way to stay up to date on New Jersey genealogy research topics. Rootsweb have an extensive listing of **New Jersey Mailing Lists** on a variety of topics.

New Jersey Mailing Lists:
http://lists.rootsweb.ancestry.com/index/usa/NJ/misc.html

New Jersey Message Boards

A message board is another internet based facility where people can post questions about a specific genealogy topic and have it answered by other genealogists. If you have questions about a surname, record type, or research topic, you can post your question and other researchers and genealogists will help you with the answer. Be sure to check back regularly, as the answers are not emailed to you. The New Jersey Message Boards at **Rootsweb** are completely free to use.

Rootsweb:
http://boards.rootsweb.com/localities.northam.usa.states/mb.ashx

New Jersey Newspapers and Periodicals

Many genealogy periodicals and historical newspapers contain reprinted copies of family genealogies, transcripts of family Bible records, information about local records and archives, census indexes, church records, queries, land records, obituaries, court records, cemetery records, and wills. The following sites have historical New Jersey newspapers and periodicals that you can search online or on-site.

New Jersey Division of Archives and Records Management – historical Newspapers 1776 – 1900s

225 West State Street
Trenton, New Jersey 08625-0307
Telephone: 609-292-6260

New Jersey Division of Archives and Records Management:
http://www.nj.gov/state/archives/index.html

New Jersey State Library - large collection of more than 2,000 periodicals plus over 70 historical and major newspapers

185 West State Street
(mailing address: P.O. Box 520)
Trenton, New Jersey 08625-0520
Telephone: 609-278-2640
Fax: 609-278-2647
E-Mail: refdesk@njstatelib.org

New Jersey State Library:
http://slic.njstatelib.org/library_collections/genealogy_and_local_his tory

GenealogyBank.com – free searchable database of New Jersey newspaper archives, 1690–2010

GenealogyBank.com:
http://www.genealogybank.com/gbnk/newspapers/explore/USA/Ne wJersey/

Library of Congress Digital Newspaper Directory – free searchable database of historical U.S. newspapers dating from 1690-present

Library of Congress Digital Newspaper Directory:
http://chroniclingamerica.loc.gov/search/titles/

NewspaperArchive.com – largest online database of historical newspapers in the world.

NewspaperArchive.com: http://newspaperarchive.com/

Historical New Jersey Maps and Gazetteers

Maps are an integral part of genealogical research. They help us to
locate landmarks, towns, cities, parishes, states, provinces,
waterways and roads and streets. They also help us to determine
when and where boundary changes might have taken place, and give
us a visualization of the area we're researching in.

For locating place names, a gazetteer is the best possible resource for
any genealogist. Gazetteers are also sometimes called "place name
dictionaries", and can help you to locate the area in which you need
to conduct research. Below are links to the maps and gazetteers for
research in New Jersey.

Peabody GNIS Service – New Jersey:
http://peabody.research.yale.edu/cgi-
bin/Query.GNIS?ST=NewJersey&SU=1

Color Landform Atlas – New Jersey:
http://fermi.jhuapl.edu/states/nj_0.html

1985 U.S. Atlas: http://www.livgenmi.com/1895/NJ/

New Jersey Hometown Locator:
http://newjersey.hometownlocator.com/

New Jersey City Directories

.

City directories are similar to telephone directories in that they list the residents of a particular area. The difference though is what is important to genealogists, and that is they pre-date telephone directories. You can find an ancestor's information such as their street address, place of employment, occupation, or the name of their spouse. A one-stop-shop for finding city directories in New Jersey is the **Montana Online Historical Directories** which contains a listing of every available online historical directory related to New Jersey.

New Jersey Online Historical Directories:
https://sites.google.com/site/onlinedirectorysite/Home/usa/nj

New Jersey State Library – hundreds of New Jersey city directories dating from early 19th century

185 West State Street
(mailing address: P.O. Box 520)
Trenton, New Jersey 08625-0520
Telephone: 609-278-2640
Fax: 609-278-2647
E-Mail: refdesk@njstatelib.org

New Jersey State Library:
http://slic.njstatelib.org/slic_files/City%20Directories.pdf

New Jersey Genealogical Records

<u>Birth, Death, Marriage and Divorce Records</u> – Also known as vital records, birth, death, and marriage certificates are the most basic, yet most important records attached to your ancestor. The reason for their importance is that they not only place your ancestor in a specific place at a definite time, but potentially connect the individual to other relatives. Below is a list of repositories and websites where you can find New Jersey vital records.

New Jersey Department of Health - Birth, marriage and death records beginning 1913, Domestic partnership records from 2004 - present, Civil union records from 2007 - present

Office of Vital Statistics and Registry
P.O. Box 370
Trenton, NJ 08625-0370

New Jersey Department of Health:
http://www.state.nj.us/health/vital/index.shtml

New Jersey Division of Archives and Records Management - New Jersey Vital Records May 1, 1848–December 31, 1912; Marriage Index, 1848-1878, Death Records, 1878-1890, Birth Corrections 1848 – 1900, Delayed Birth Certificates 1848 – 1900, County records of Births of Slave Children in 1804, microfilm copies of the Department of Health records for Births: January 1, 1913–December 31, 1923, Marriages: January 1, 1913–December 31, 1940, Deaths: January 1, 1913–December 31, 1955, Pre-1848 Marriage Records, Colonial Marriages, 1665-1799, Divorces 1743-1880's

225 West State Street
Trenton, New Jersey 08625-0307
Telephone: 609-292-6260

New Jersey Division of Archives and Records Management:
http://www.nj.gov/state/archives/index.html

Family Search has the following indexes which can be searched online for free:

1. **New Jersey Deaths and Burials, 1720-1988**
2. **New Jersey, Births and Christenings, 1660-1980**
3. **New Jersey, County Marriages, 1682-1956**
4. **New Jersey, Marriages, 1678-1985**

New Jersey Deaths and Burials, 1720-1988:
https://familysearch.org/search/collection/1675445

New Jersey, Births and Christenings, 1660-1980:
https://familysearch.org/search/collection/1675383

New Jersey, County Marriages, 1682-1956:
https://familysearch.org/search/collection/1803976

New Jersey, Marriages, 1678-1985:
https://familysearch.org/search/collection/1675446

<u>Census Reports</u>

Census records are among the most important genealogical documents for placing your ancestor in a particular place at a specific time. Like BDM records, they can also lead you to other ancestors, particularly those who were living under the authority of the head of household.
Census records:
http://obituarieshelp.org/utilizing_census_returns.html

Federal census records for New Jersey exist from 1830–1940 and can be found at:

New Jersey Division of Archives and Records Management -
Federal Censuses 1830-1940, State Censuses 1855-1915

225 West State Street
Trenton, New Jersey 08625-0307
Telephone: 609-292-6260

New Jersey Division of Archives and Records Management:
http://www.nj.gov/state/archives/index.html

National Archives – Federal census Schedules for all states, 1790-1940

8601 Adelphi Road
College Park, MD 20740-6001
Tel: 1-866-272-6272

National Archives: http://www.archives.gov/research/census/

The **Free Census Project** has transcribed many New Jersey indexes and new material is added daily

Free Census Project: http://usgwcensus.org/cenfiles/nj.htm

Access Genealogy – New Jersey county census records from 1800-1930

Access Genealogy: http://www.accessgenealogy.com/census/new-jersey-census-records.htm

African American Census Schedules Online – slave schedules, mortality schedules, slave-owners census

African American Census Schedules Online: http://www.afrigeneas.com/aacensus/ga/

Native Americans in Census Records (US National Archives)

Native Americans in Census Records: http://www.archives.gov/research/census/native-americans/

New Jersey Church Records

Church and synagogue records are a valuable resource, especially for baptisms, marriages, and burials that took place before 1900. You will need to at least have an idea of your ancestor's religious denomination, and in most cases you will have to visit a brick and mortar establishment to view them.

Most church records are kept by the individual church, although in some denominations, records are placed in a regional archive or maintained at the diocesan level. Local Historical Societies are sometimes the repository for the state's older church records. Below are links archives that maintain church records, as well as a few databases that can be viewed online.

The **Family History Library** contains many church records from a variety of denominations on microfilm.

Family History Library:
http://familysearch.org/learn/wiki/en/Family_History_Library

Gloucester County Historical Society Library – large collection of multi-denominational church records from New Jersey and the rest of the United States

17 Hunter Street
Woodbury, New Jersey 08096-4605
Telephone: 856-845-4771

Gloucester County Historical Society Library:
http://www.rootsweb.ancestry.com/~njgchs/PDF/Church.pdf

Central Repositories for Denominational Records

Church of Jesus Christ of Latter-day Saints (Mormons)

Early Mormon Church records for Montana can be found on film located at the LDS Family History Library in Salt Lake City and can be searched via the **Family History Library Catalog**

Family History Library Catalog:
https://familysearch.org/eng/Library/FHLC/frameset_fhlc.asp

Baptist

American Baptist Historical Society
3001 Mercer University Dr.
Atlanta, Georgia 30341
Telephone: (678) 547-6680

American Baptist Historical Society: http://abhsarchives.org/

Dutch Reformed

Commission on History, Reformed Church in America
New Brunswick Theological Seminary
Gardner A. Sage Library
21 Seminary Place
New Brunswick, New Jersey 08901
Telephone: (732) 246-1779

Gardner A. Sage Library:
https://www.rca.org/sslpage.aspx?pid=230

Episcopal

Diocesan House of the Episcopal Church
808 W. State Street
Trenton, New Jersey 08618-5326
Telephone: (609) 394-5281

Diocesan House of the Episcopal Church:
http://www.newjersey.anglican.org/ECUSA/index.html

Jewish - Synagogue and cemetery records for some congregations in Middlesex, Somerset, and Union counties are at:

Jewish Historical Society of Central Jersey
1050 George St, Box 1-L
New Brunswick, New Jersey 08901
Telephone: (732) 249-4894

Jewish Historical Society of Central Jersey:
http://www.jewishgen.org/jhscj/index.html

Methodist

United Methodist Church
Commission on Archives and History
Greater New Jersey Conference
1001 Wickapecko Drive
Ocean, New Jersey 07712
Phone: (732) 359-1000; Toll free: (877) 677-2594

Greater New Jersey Conference:
http://www.gnjumc.org/pages/detail/293

Presbyterian

Presbyterian Historical Society
United Presbyterian Church in the USA
425 Lombard Street
Philadelphia, Pennsylvania 19147
Telephone: (215) 627-1852

Presbyterian Historical Society: http://www.history.pcusa.org/

Roman Catholic

Diocese of Camden
631 Market Street
Camden, New Jersey 08102
Phone: (856) 756-7900.

Diocese of Camden: http://www.camdendiocese.org/

Diocese of Metuchen
P.O. Box 191
Metuchen, NJ 08840-0191
Phone: (732) 562-1990
Office Location
146 Metlars Lane
Piscataway, New Jersey 08854

Diocese of Metuchen : http://diometuchen.org/

Archdiocese of Newark
171 Clifton Avenue
Newark, New Jersey 07104-0500
C/O University Archives
Seton Hall University
South Orange Avenue
South Orange, New Jersey 07079
Phone: (201) 762-7052

University Archives:
http://www.shu.edu/academics/libraries/archives/newark-archdiocese.cfm

The Roman Catholic Diocese of Paterson
777 Valley Road
Paterson, New Jersey 07013
Phone: (973) 777-8818

The Roman Catholic Diocese of Paterson:
http://www.patersondiocese.org/index.cfm

Diocese of Trenton
701 Lawrenceville Road
Trenton, New Jersey 08648
Phone: (609) 406-7400

Diocese of Trenton : http://www.dioceseoftrenton.org/

Society of Friends (Quakers)

The Friends Historical Library
Swarthmore College
500 College Avenue
Swarthmore, Pennsylvania 19801
Telephone: (610) 328-8496

The Friends Historical Library:
http://www.swarthmore.edu/academics/friends-historical-library.xml

New Jersey Military Records

More than 40 million Americans have participated in some time of war service since America was colonized. The chance of finding your ancestor amongst those records is exceptionally high. Military records can even reveal individuals who never actually served, such as those who registered for the two World Wars but were never called to duty.

Below are a number of links to websites and archives that contain New Jersey military records.

New Jersey Division of Archives and Records Management - Colonial Wars records 1639-c.1775, Revolutionary War records 1776-1783, War of 1812 records (Records of Officers and Men of New Jersey in Wars 1791-1815 and Pensions 1874-1900), Civil War records, Punitive Expedition to Mexico muster rolls 1916, WWI service cards 1917-1918

225 West State Street
Trenton, New Jersey 08625-0307
Telephone: 609-292-6260

New Jersey Division of Archives and Records Management:
http://www.nj.gov/state/archives/index.html

National Archives - Northeast Region – Draft, Military Service, and Pension and Bounty Land Application Files

201 Varick Street
12th Floor
New York, New York 10014
Telephone: Toll-free 866-840-1752 or 212-401-1620
Fax: 212-401-1638

National Archives - Northeast Region:
http://www.archives.gov/nyc/public/genealogy.html

United States General Index to Pension Files, 1861-1934

United States General Index to Pension Files, 1861-1934:
https://familysearch.org/search/collection/1919699

United States Index to Service Records, War with Spain, 1898

United States Index to Service Records, War with Spain, 1898:
https://familysearch.org/search/collection/1919583

United States Index to Indian Wars Pension Files, 1892-1926 – military pension records of soldiers who fought in the Indian Wars between 1817 and 1898

United States Index to Indian Wars Pension Files, 1892-1926:
https://familysearch.org/search/collection/1979427

United States Registers of Enlistments in the U.S. Army, 1798-1914 - index of men who enlisted in the United States Army, 1798-1914.

United States Registers of Enlistments in the U.S. Army, 1798-1914: https://familysearch.org/search/collection/1880762

United States Mexican War Pension Index, 1887-1926 - index to Mexican War pension files for service between 1846 and 1848

United States Mexican War Pension Index, 1887-1926:
https://familysearch.org/search/collection/1979390

Civil War Soldiers Service Records - Service records for both Union and Confederate soldiers indexed by soldier's name, rank, and unit.

Civil War Soldier Service Records:
http://go.fold3.com/civilwar_records/

New Jersey Cemetery Records

As convenient as it is to search cemetery records online, keep in mind that there are a few disadvantages over visiting a cemetery in person. They are:

- Tombstone information is not always accurately transcribed
- The arrangement of the graves in a cemetery can be crucial as family members are often buried next to each other or in the same grave. This arrangement is not always preserved in the alphabetical indexes that are found online.

With that information in mind, the following websites have databases that can be searched online for New Jersey Cemetery records.

Genealogical Society of New Jersey – cemetery records and gravestone transcriptions from many New Jersey cemeteries

PO Box 1476
Trenton, NJ 08607-1476

Genealogical Society of New Jersey:
http://www.rootsweb.ancestry.com/~njgsnj/collectionguide.html

New Jersey Tombstone Transcription Project - death and burial records

New Jersey Tombstone Transcription Project:
http://www.usgwtombstones.org/newjer/newjer.html

African American Cemeteries Online – African American, slave, and Native American cemetery records

African American Cemeteries Online:
http://africanamericancemeteries.com/ar/

Access Genealogy – database of New Jersey cemetery record transcriptions

Access Genealogy:
http://www.accessgenealogy.com/cemetery/new-jersey-cemetery-records.htm

US Department of Veterans Affairs Nationwide Gravesite Locator – includes information on veterans and their family members buried in veterans and military cemeteries having a government grave marker.

US Department of Veterans Affairs Nationwide Gravesite Locator: http://gravelocator.cem.va.gov/

Find a Grave – over 100 million grave records can be searched on this site. Search can be conducted by name, location, or cemetery name.

Find a Grave: http://www.findagrave.com/

Interment.net - A free online database containing approximately 4 million cemetery records from around the world.

Interment.net: http://www.interment.net/

Billion Graves – as the name implies, you can search a billion records including headstone photos, transcriptions, cemetery records, and grave locations.

Billion Graves:
http://billiongraves.com/pages/search/index.php#cemetery

New Jersey Obituaries

Obituaries can reveal a wealth about our ancestor and other relatives. You can search our **New Jersey Newspaper Obituaries Listings** from hundreds of New Jersey newspapers online for free.

New Jersey Newspaper Obituaries Listings link to: http://obituarieshelp.org/new_jersey_newspaper_obituaries.html

New Jersey Wills and Probate Records

The documents found in a probate packet may include a complete inventory of a person's estate, newspaper entries, witness testimony, a copy of a will, list of debtors and creditors, names of executors or trustees, names of heirs. They can not only tell you about the ancestor you're currently researching, but lead to other ancestors.

Because of its history New Jersey has a complicated probate scenario, and records can be hard to find. From 1702 to 1738 New York and New Jersey had the same governor resulting many New Jersey probate records held among **New York City**, or **Albany** probate records. The prerogative court began probating New Jersey wills and administrations in 1670, the governor holding authority over probates until 1844.

Probates for East and West Jersey continued to be recorded in Perth Amboy and Burlington until 1784 when the secretary of state became the register of the prerogative court, and all original records from then on have been sent to his office in Trenton. Those records can be found at:

New Jersey Division of Archives and Records Management – vital records, census records, land and estate records, tax records, military records, court records, naturalization records, historical newspapers collection

225 West State Street
Trenton, New Jersey 08625-0307
Telephone: 609-292-6260

New Jersey Division of Archives and Records Management:
http://www.nj.gov/state/archives/index.html

Genealogical Society of New Jersey – Index to Slaves and Servants in the New Jersey Calendar of Wills 1670-1817

PO Box 1476
Trenton, NJ 08607-1476

Genealogical Society of New Jersey:
http://www.rootsweb.ancestry.com/~njgchs/PDF/slaves.pdf

Family Search has the following indexes that can be searched online for free:

New Jersey, Middlesex County Probate Records, 1830-1921 link to: https://familysearch.org/search/collection/1973535

New Jersey, Probate Records, 1678-1980:
https://familysearch.org/search/collection/2018330

New Jersey Immigration and Naturalization Records

The naturalization process generated many types of records, including petitions, declarations of intention, and oaths of allegiance. These records can provide family historians with information such as a person's birth date and place of birth, immigration year, marital status, spouse information, occupation, witnesses' names and addresses, and more.

New Jersey Division of Archives and Records Management – naturalizations 1790-1960

225 West State Street
Trenton, New Jersey 08625-0307
Telephone: 609-292-6260

New Jersey Division of Archives and Records Management:
http://www.nj.gov/state/archives/index.html

National Archives - Northeast Region - Naturalization Records, Passenger Arrival Lists, Canadian Border Entry Records, Customs Records, Chinese Exclusion Act Case Files, Freedmen's Bureau and Records Pertaining to African American Families, Dawes Commission Final Cards of the Five Civilized Tribes

201 Varick Street
12th Floor
New York, New York 10014
Telephone: Toll-free 866-840-1752 or 212-401-1620
Fax: 212-401-1638

National Archives - Northeast Region:
http://www.archives.gov/nyc/public/genealogy.html

U.S. National Archives – Immigration and Naturalization records, 1787-1993

U.S. National Archives: http://www.archives.gov/research/guide-fed-records/groups/085.html

New Jersey Native American Records

National Archives - Northeast Region - Dawes Commission Final Cards of the Five Civilized Tribes

201 Varick Street
12th Floor
New York, New York 10014
Telephone: Toll-free 866-840-1752 or 212-401-1620
Fax: 212-401-1638

National Archives - Northeast Region:
http://www.archives.gov/nyc/public/genealogy.html

Access Genealogy – New Jersey Native American census records, tribal histories, and much more

Access Genealogy: http://www.accessgenealogy.com/native/new-jersey-indian-tribes.htm

U.S. National Archives - information on American Indians who maintained their ties to Federally-recognized Tribes (1830-1970).

U.S. National Archives: http://www.archives.gov/research/native-americans/

Records of the Bureau of Indian Affairs (BIA)

Records of the Bureau of Indian Affairs (BIA):
http://www.archives.gov/research/guide-fed-records/groups/075.html

American Indians Records Repository - records dating from the 1700s including trust, education and other historic Indian Affairs records

American Indian Records Repository
Meritex Enterprises
17501 West 98th Street
Lenexa, KS 66219
Phone: 913-888-0601

American Indians Records Repository:
http://www.doi.gov/ost/records_mgmt/american-indian-records-repository.cfm

Missing Matriarchs – Resources for Researching Female New Jersey Ancestors

Looking for female ancestors requires an adjustment of how we view traditional records sources. A woman's identity was often under that of her husband, and often individual records for them can be difficult to locate. The following resources are effective in locating female ancestors in New Jersey where traditional records may not reveal them.

<u>Bibliographies</u>

- *Past and Promise: Lives of New Jersey Women,* Margaret Cook (Journal of Rutgers University Library, 1971)
- *Fortunes of War: New Jersey Women and the American Revolution,* Linda G. DePauw (New Jersey Historical Commission, 1975)
- *New Jersey Quilts, 1777 to 1950: Contributions to an American Tradition,* Heritage Quilt Project of New Jersey, (American Quilters Society, 1992)

Selected Resources for New Jersey Women's History

Messler Library
Farleigh Dickinson University
Montross Ave.
Rutherford, NJ 07070

Special Collections and Archives
Rutgers University
New Brunswick, NJ 08903

Common New Jersey Surnames

The following surnames are among the most common in New Jersey and are also being currently researched by other genealogists. If you find your surname here, there is a chance that some research has already been performed on your ancestor.

Acolia, Ahearn, Aldrich, Alpaugh, Apgar, Applegate, Ayers, Barker, Barnes, Baxter, Beecher, Bishop, Bissel, Blakeslee, Bliss, Bloom, Bonham, Borton, Bradbury, Brown, Burd, Burke, Burns, Butler, Cahill, Campbell, Carolan, Carson, Cervenka, Chamberlain, Champlain, Chapman, Chappell, Cheregothis, Cherry, Chludzinski, Church, Cockestarles, Conklin, Conlin, Cook, Coppock, Corbishley, Cottrell, Crammer, Crampton, Creighton, Creighton, Cross, Cunningham, Curtis, Davidson, Davis, Demuth, Dennis, Derr, Diehl, Doran, Downer, DuBois, Dufford, Earlin, Earling, Eckert, Edwards, Ehret, Eick, Elliot, Ellis, Emery, Emhardt, English, Erwin, Evans, Faulkner, Finnegan, Focht, Follett, Folz, Foret, Fowler, Franklin, Freeburger, Frome, Fuchs, Fuhrmann, Geer, Glen, Glenn, Goeke, Goeller, Gotwals, Grace, Grau, Gray, Griswold, Gross, Haag, Hahn, Haines, Hallisy, Halsey, Hancock, Handshuch, Harger, Harney, Hickey, Highfield, Hillig, Holcombe, Holden, Horn, Howarth, Hutchinson, Hyde, Jansson, Jezabek, Johnson, Jones, Katz, Kemp, Kightlinyer, Knox, Korzun, Kotowski, Libby, Lightsky, Lindsey, MacCauley, Mack, Mackey, Maddalena, Malsbury, Maltby, Mansier, Mansir, Masters, May, McBride, McCollum, McCrelis, McCullough, McGill, McHugh, McKeown, McKinney, McNally, McPeek, Meier, Melick, Miller, Mooney, Morris, Morton, Mowbry, Murdock, Murphy, Myers, Nagy, Navatkoski, Needham, Nowatkowski, O'Harrow, Oberlin, Oberly, Olds, Ott, Park, Parke, Parker, Partlow, Percy, Perrin, Perrine, Phelps, Philhower, Phillips, Pickell, Pinney, Pirigyi, Pittman, Pogorzelski, Poland, Potter, Powell, Pownell, Price, Radline, Redlne, Reeder, Rege, Rice, Rich, Richardson, Rosenwig, Rosenzweig, Rosewig, Rudy, Runyon, Ryno,

Salmons, Saxton, Schaefer, Schmidt, Sclover, Scott, Seaman, Searl, Shaeffer, Sheaffer, Sheets, Shine, Shippe, Sly, Smith, Spellman, Springfield, Stainbrook, Staszewski, Stavrakos, Sparta, Stehzerin, Steven, Stout, Stratton, Swackhammer, Sweezey, Taylor, Thomas, Tichenor, Tomlinson, Torry, Tory, Tripp, Tuohy, Vela, Waggoner, Wagner, Walsh, Walter, Walters, Warren, Waters, Webb, Weleh,

About the Author

Gary L. Morris worked from 2009 to 2014 as a professional researcher for a major player in the genealogy field. After tracing his family lineage back to 1683, he found that genealogy could be an expensive undertaking. As such, has decided to publish these helpful guides to share the valuable free information he has discovered during his career to help others trace their family lineages as inexpensively as possible. An avid genealogist himself, he hopes you will find this guide factual,

www.ingramcontent.com/pod-product-compliance
Lightning Source LLC
Chambersburg PA
CBHW061927280526
45787CB00004B/1511